Ocean Moments
Mindfulness Scenes for Kids

Little Soul Inc.

What is Mindfulness?

Mindfulness is paying close attention to the present moment, noticing everything around and within you. It's like using a magnifying glass on your thoughts and feelings, helping you feel calm, focused, and happy.

In this book, you'll explore various ocean scenes to practice mindfulness, each with a task to help you notice details and imagine more with your eyes closed.

Enjoy your journey through peaceful scenes, have fun with the activities, and take your time to notice everything. Being mindful helps you feel calm, happy, and connected to the world.

Have Fun and Be Mindful!

Underwater World

Imagine you are a fish swimming peacefully in this beautiful underwater world. The water is cool and calm, and you can see the sunlight dancing on the ocean floor.

As you swim slowly through the clear water, you notice the gentle movements of the seaweed and the soft colors of the coral. The little fish around you are your friends, and they swim with you, making you feel safe and happy.

Take a deep breath in and imagine you are floating just like these fish, feeling light and free. Let your mind be as calm as the water, and whenever you feel a little worried, remember this peaceful ocean where everything is quiet and still. You can always come back to this place in your mind to feel relaxed and at ease.

Shoreline

Imagine standing on the shore by the ocean. The ground beneath your feet is made of smooth, round stones, and you can hear the gentle sound of waves washing over them. The cool breeze carries the fresh scent of the sea, and the sky is soft with fluffy clouds.

As you look out at the ocean, you notice the waves calmly rolling in, splashing against the rocks in a soothing rhythm. Small tide pools are scattered around, each one a tiny world filled with clear water and little sea creatures.

Take a deep breath, feeling the cool air and listening to the calming sounds of the waves. Let your mind be as peaceful as the ocean. Whenever you need to find calm, think of this quiet shore where everything feels peaceful and safe.

Shallow Pond

Imagine standing by a shallow pond in the ocean. The water is clear and calm, with a soft green colour that lets you see the sandy bottom below. Gentle waves surround the pond, softly touching the sandy shore.

Sunlight shines down, creating beautiful patterns of light that dance on the surface of the water. Small fish swim calmly through the pond, their movements slow and peaceful.

As you watch the scene, take a deep breath and feel the tranquility of this special place. Let your mind be as still as the calm water, and whenever you need to relax, imagine yourself by this serene ocean pond, where everything is quiet and peaceful.

Dolphin Leaping

Imagine being underwater, where everything is calm and peaceful. The water is a beautiful blue, and soft beams of sunlight filter through the surface, creating gentle patterns all around you.

In the distance, you see a dolphin gracefully leaping out of the water. Its smooth, playful movements fill you with a sense of joy and freedom. As you watch the dolphin, you feel connected to the calmness of the ocean and the beauty of the moment.

Take a deep breath, and let the peacefulness of this scene fill your mind. Whenever you need to feel relaxed, picture this dolphin leaping joyfully in the serene, blue water.

Gentle Waves at Sunrise

Imagine standing on a quiet beach as the sun begins to rise. The sky is painted with soft colors—pinks, oranges, and purples—spreading warmth across the horizon. The gentle waves roll in, one after another, softly touching the shore.

The sound of the waves is soothing, like a gentle heartbeat, and the cool morning air feels refreshing on your skin. The sunlight reflects off the water, creating a path of golden light that stretches out to the horizon.

As you watch the sunrise, take a deep breath and let the peacefulness of this moment fill you. Let your thoughts flow as smoothly as the waves, and whenever you need to find calm, picture this beautiful sunrise and the gentle waves that bring a sense of peace.

Sailboat on the Horizon

Imagine standing on a quiet beach, looking out at the big, wide ocean. The water is calm, with little waves that ripple when the soft wind blows. Far away, you can see a small sailboat, its white sails shining in the sun as it gently moves across the water.

The sailboat moves slowly and smoothly, making everything feel quiet and peaceful. The sky is clear, with a few fluffy clouds floating by. Seeing the tiny sailboat on the big ocean makes you think about the gentle path of life.

As you watch the sailboat, take a deep breath and feel the peace of this moment. Let your mind drift as calmly as the boat on the water, and whenever you need to relax, imagine this peaceful ocean scene, where everything moves at a gentle, soothing pace.

Turtles Paradise

Imagine being underwater in a calm, blue ocean, where the water is clear and still. Around you, gentle sea turtles glide gracefully through the water, their movements slow and peaceful. The turtles move easily, their flippers gently pushing them forward as they swim.

Sunlight filters down from above, creating soft, glowing patterns on the ocean floor. The water is quiet, with only the soft sound of bubbles rising to the surface. The turtles swim together, their presence bringing a sense of calm.

As you watch the turtles, take a deep breath and feel the peacefulness of this underwater world. Let your thoughts slow down, just like the turtles, and whenever you need to find calm, imagine yourself swimming alongside these gentle creatures in the ocean.

Jellyfish

Imagine floating in a quiet, blue ocean, where everything is calm and serene. Around you, graceful jellyfish move slowly through the water. Their delicate, translucent bodies move with the current.

The jellyfish are surrounded by soft beams of sunlight that filter through the water, casting a gentle glow around them. They move in a slow, rhythmic dance, their long, flowing tentacles trailing behind them like ribbons.

As you watch the jellyfish, take a deep breath and feel the peace of this underwater world. Let your mind be as light and free as the jellyfish, and whenever you need to relax, imagine yourself drifting alongside these gentle creatures, surrounded by the calm and beauty of the ocean.

Coral

Imagine yourself exploring a vibrant coral reef beneath the clear, blue ocean. The water is warm and gentle, making you feel safe and relaxed. All around you, colourful coral sway softly with the current, like underwater gardens filled with life.

Tiny fish of every colour swim gracefully between the coral, their movements calm and soothing. The sunlight filters down through the water, casting a warm, golden glow on everything it touches. You can see the patterns of light dancing on the sandy ocean floor, creating a beautiful and peaceful scene.

As you watch the coral and the fish, take a deep breath in and feel the peace of this underwater world. Let your mind be as calm as the gentle waves, and whenever you need to relax, remember this serene coral reef where everything is quiet, colorful, and full of life.

Kelp Forest

Imagine yourself gliding through an underwater kelp forest. Tall, green kelp plants reach up towards the sunlight, swaying gently with the ocean current. The water is clear and cool, and beams of sunlight filter through the leaves.

Small fish swim among the kelp, their movements slow and calming. The gentle rustle of the kelp and the soft bubbling of the water make you feel relaxed and safe.

Take a deep breath in, feeling the cool, refreshing water around you. Let your mind be as calm as the swaying kelp, and whenever you need to find peace, imagine yourself in this quiet, soothing underwater forest.

Quiet Cove

Imagine being in a quiet cove beneath the ocean's surface. The water is clear and calm, with a soft blue-green hue that makes you feel peaceful and safe. Around you, the sandy ocean floor is dotted with smooth rocks and gentle patches of seagrass that sway slowly with the current.

The cove is a hidden, tranquil place where everything moves in slow, soothing rhythms. Small fish swim among the rocks, their colors blending with the peaceful surroundings. Sunlight filters through the water, creating soft, shimmering patterns that dance on the sand.

As you take in this scene, breathe deeply and feel the calmness of this quiet cove. Let your mind be as still as the water, and whenever you need to find peace, picture yourself in this serene underwater sanctuary, where everything is quiet, gentle, and safe.

Polar Underwater Scene

Imagine diving into the icy, clear waters of the polar regions. The water is a deep blue, and you see sunlight shining through the ice, creating magical patterns on the ocean floor.

Around you, tall ice formations rise like giant towers. The water is calm, with small bubbles slowly rising to the surface. You might see graceful fish swimming by, moving slowly as if they're in no hurry.

The cold water feels refreshing, making you aware of each breath you take. This peaceful underwater world helps you feel calm and relaxed. Whenever you need to feel centered, picture this quiet, serene place.

Underwater Cave

Imagine exploring a hidden underwater cave deep in the ocean. The water around you is cool and clear, with a soft blue tint that makes everything feel calm and mysterious. As you enter the cave, you notice the walls are lined with smooth, ancient rocks, gently illuminated by beams of light that filter through small openings above.

The cave is peaceful and quiet, with only the sound of your breathing and the soft movement of the water around you. Tiny fish dart in and out of the shadows, their movements slow and graceful. The cave feels like a safe place where time seems to stand still.

As you take in the beauty of this underwater cave, breathe deeply and feel the deep sense of calm it brings. Let your thoughts become as still as the water inside the cave, and whenever you need to relax, imagine yourself in this tranquil underwater world, where everything is quiet, safe, and full of wonder.

Stormy Sea

Imagine standing by the edge of a stormy ocean. The sky above is dark and full of swirling clouds, and the wind whips through the air, carrying the scent of salt and rain. The waves crash against the shore with powerful energy.

Even in the storm's intensity, there is a rhythm—a steady, unbreakable pattern in the way the waves move. As you watch, you notice how the storm stirs the ocean, but beneath the surface, the water is calm and deep.

Take a deep breath and feel the energy of the storm around you. Let it remind you that, like the ocean, you can find calm within, even when life feels chaotic. Whenever you need to find your inner peace, think of the powerful waves and the quiet strength of the deep ocean beneath them.

Whale Watching

Imagine being in the vast, open ocean, where the water is deep and calm. In the distance, you see a majestic whale gracefully gliding through the water. Its enormous body moves slowly and powerfully, each movement smooth and effortless. The whale's presence brings a sense of awe and peace.

As the whale swims, you hear the soft, melodic sound of its calls echoing through the water. The sound is deep and soothing, like a lullaby from the ocean itself. The whale occasionally rises to the surface, sending up a gentle spray of water before diving back down into the deep blue.

As you watch the whale, take a deep breath and feel the tranquility of this moment. Let your thoughts flow as calmly as the whale moves through the water. Whenever you need to find peace, imagine yourself alongside this gentle giant in the serene, endless ocean.

www.ingramcontent.com/pod-product-compliance
Lightning Source LLC
LaVergne TN
LVHW072125070426
835511LV00003B/90

9 781777 596675